GETTING TO KNOW THE WORLD'S GREATEST ARTISTS

J A C O B
LAWRENCE

WRITTEN AND ILLUSTRATED BY MIKE VENEZIA

CHILDREN'S PRESS®
A DIVISION OF GROLIER PUBLISHING
NEW YORK   LONDON   HONG KONG   SYDNEY
DANBURY, CONNECTICUT

Cover: *Harriet Tubman Series No. 10,* by Jacob Lawrence. 1939-40. Casein tempera on gessoed hardboard. 17 7/8 x 12 in. © Hampton University Museum, Hampton, VA.

Colorist for illustrations: Kathy Hickey

Library of Congress Cataloging-in-Publication Data

Venezia, Mike.
    Jacob Lawrence / written and illustrated by Mike Venezia.
        p. cm. — (Getting to know the world's greatest artists)
    Summary: A biography of the African-American painter who used his
art to tell stories about the lives of individual Blacks and historical events
important in the lives of his people.
    ISBN 0-516-21012-2 (lib.bdg.)   0-516-26533-4(pbk)
    1. Lawrence, Jacob, 1917-   Juvenile literature. 2. Afro-American painters Biography.
[1. Lawrence, Jacob, 1917-   . 2. Afro-Americans Biography.   3. Afro-Americans in art.
4. Artists. 5. Art appreciation. 6. Painting, American.] I. Title. II. Series:
Venezia, Mike. Getting to know the world's greatest artists.
N6537.L384V   1999
791.13—dc21
    [B]   99-13840
                                                                      CIP
                                                                       AC

Self-Portrait, by Jacob Lawrence. 1977. Gouache on paper. 23 x 31 in.
© National Academy of Design/Photograph by Glenn Castellano.

Jacob Lawrence was born in 1917 in Atlantic City, New Jersey. He loved using art to tell stories. Jacob's paintings often show important historical events, but he liked to paint scenes of everyday life, too.

Deception (Toussaint L'Ouverture series), by Jacob Lawrence. 1997. Screenprint. 22 1/4 x 32 3/16 in.
© Courtesy of the Artist and Francine Seders Gallery/Photograph by Richard Nicol.

Some of the historical stories Jacob Lawrence painted were the exciting adventures of African-American heros. Toussaint L'Ouverture, for example, was a slave on the island of Haiti. He managed to organize other slaves into an excellent army who fought their French rulers to win freedom.

Harriet Tubman Series No. 10, by Jacob Lawrence. 1939-40. Casein tempera on gessoed hardboard. 17 7/8 x 12 in. © Hampton University Museum, Hampton, VA.

Harriet Tubman was a slave in the state of Maryland. She escaped from her owners, but risked her life over and over again by returning to the South to help other slaves escape.

Because there was so much to know about the exciting people Jacob portrayed, he usually painted lots of scenes for each story. He also would write a few sentences for each painting to help explain what was going on in the scene.

John Brown Series No. 2: "For 40 years, John Brown reflected on the hopeless and miserable condition of the slaves," by Jacob Lawrence. 1941. Gouache on white wove. 50.8 x 35.6 cm. Gift of Mr. and Mrs. Milton Lowenthal. © The Detroit Institute of Arts.

John Brown Series No. 6: "John Brown formed an organization among the colored people of the Adirondack Woods to resist the capture of any fugitive slaves," by Jacob Lawrence. 1941. Gouache on white wove. 50.8 x 35.6 cm. Gift of Mr. and Mrs. Milton Lowenthal. © The Detroit Institute of Arts.

John Brown Series No. 12: "*John Brown's victory at Black Jack drove those pro-slavery to new fury, and those who were anti-slavery to new efforts,*" by Jacob Lawrence. 1941. Gouache on white wove. 50.8 x 35.6 cm. Gift of Mr. and Mrs. Milton Lowenthal. © The Detroit Institute of Arts.

John Brown Series No. 17: "*John Brown remained a full winter in Canada, drilling negroes for his coming raid on Harper's Ferry,*" by Jacob Lawrence. 1941. Gouache on white wove. 50.8 x 35.6 cm. Gift of Mr. and Mrs. Milton Lowenthal. © The Detroit Institute of Arts.

Rooftops (No. 1, This Is Harlem), by Jacob Lawrence. 1942-43. Gouache with pencil underdrawing on paper. 15 3/8 x 22 11/16 in. Gift of Joseph H. Hirshhorn, 1966. © Hirshhorn Museum and Sculpture Garden, Smithsonian Institution/Photograph by Lee Stalsworth.

Jacob got ideas for other paintings from watching everyday events in his neighborhood. When Jacob was thirteen, his family moved to a section of New York City called Harlem. At first, Jacob couldn't believe how crowded the streets were and how tall the buildings seemed.

Harlem was a place where African Americans could live without being treated badly, as they were in many parts of the U.S. at this time. Even though Harlem was overcrowded and jobs were hard to find, black people felt more comfortable there.

Chocolate Soda Wagon, 1928. Photograph by James VanDerZee. © Donna M. VanDerZee.

Jacob Lawrence lived in Harlem with his mother, younger brother, and sister. Jacob's father had left the family years before. To keep her children out of trouble while she was working, Mrs. Lawrence entered them in a type of day-care center called a settlement house.

This was where Jacob first became interested in art. The center had lots of arts-and-crafts activities. Jacob started working with crayons and poster paints. He got ideas for his first paintings from all the colorful patterns that decorated his family's apartment.

Next, Jacob started painting street scenes on cardboard boxes. He would cut a cardboard box apart and use three sides of it to get a three-dimensional look.

Because his mother was always working and his father wasn't around, Jacob got most of his encouragement, self-confidence, and inspiration from the people and sights of Harlem. It was almost as if the neighborhood were his family.

Artists who helped run neighborhood art programs in Harlem could see right away that Jacob Lawrence had unusual talent. They knew how serious and hardworking Jacob was, and they helped him as much as possible. But Jacob Lawrence learned about art mostly on his own. He read lots of art books and listened to older artists discuss their work.

Stela of the steward Montuwosre. Egyptian, c. 1955 B.C. Painted limestone. 41 x 19 5/8 in. Gift of Edward S. Harkness, 1912. © Metropolitan Museum of Art.

The Epiphany, by Giotto di Bondone. Tempera on wood, gold ground. 17 3/4 x 17 1/4 in. John Stewart Kennedy Fund, 1911. © Metropolitan Museum of Art.

Zapatistas, by José Clemente Orozco. 1931. Oil on canvas. 45 x 55 in. Given anonymously.
© Museum of Modern Art, New York/Photograph 2000.

Jacob visited as many art museums in New York City as he could. He saw how both ancient and modern artists used colors and shapes, and how they told their stories.

While Jacob was studying art, he also became interested in African-American history. A history teacher suggested that Jacob see a special exhibition of African sculpture at the Museum of Modern Art. It was an important trip for Jacob. He was fascinated by how much expression and power there was in the faces of the sculptures. Jacob was inspired by these mysterious statues and tried to show the same kind of expression in his own masklike faces.

(Top) Mask. Kuba related peoples, Zaire, by unknown artist. Wood, pigment. 24 in. Private Collection © Art Resource, NY/Photograph by Aldo Tutino.

(Left) Container. Mangbetu peoples, Zaire, by unknown artist. Wood, bark. 20 1/2 in. © Art Resource, NY/Photograph by Aldo Tutino.

Street Orator, by Jacob Lawrence. Gouache on paper. 23 1/4 x 18 in. © Courtesy of the Artist and Francine Seders Gallery/Photograph by Paul Macapia.

"In the North the African American had more educational opportunities." Panel 58 from *The Migration Series,*
by Jacob Lawrence. 1940-41; text and title revised by the artist, 1993. Tempera on gesso on composition board.
12 x 18 in. Gift of Mrs. David M. Levy © Museum of Modern Art, New York/Photograph 2000.

African-American history was hardly
ever taught in schools when Jacob
Lawrence was young. Jacob thought this
was a serious problem. He knew that
people who didn't know about their history
had no way of feeling proud of their past
or of themselves.

Jacob thought he might be able to help change this with his art. He began by painting the *Toussaint L'Ouverture* series. It contained forty-one pictures. They were shown at a local gallery and got lots of attention right away. People liked the way Jacob created a clear, honest story using flat, simple shapes and colors.

The Capture (Toussaint L'Ouverture series), by Jacob Lawrence. Screenprint, 1987. 32 1/8 x 22 in. © Courtesy of the Artist and Francine Seders Gallery/Photograph by Spike Mafford.

Harriet Tubman Series No. 7, by Jacob Lawrence. 1939-40. Casein tempera on gessoed hardboard. 17 7/8 x 12 in. © Hampton University Museum, Hampton, VA.

Next, Jacob painted his series about Harriet Tubman. Then he did a series on Frederick Douglass. Frederick Douglass had escaped slavery, too. After working hard to educate himself, he started a successful newspaper. Frederick Douglass spent his life fighting slavery, and became a United States Marshall.

Frederick Douglass Series No. 21, by Jacob Lawrence. 1938-39. Casein tempera on gessoed hardboard. 17 7/8 x 12 in. © Hampton University Museum, Hampton, VA.

Frederick Douglass Series No. 13, by Jacob Lawrence. 1938-39. Casein tempera on gessoed hardboard. 17 7/8 x 12 in. © Hampton University Museum, Hampton, VA.

One of Jacob's most popular series was *The Migration Series*. It's made up of sixty paintings! It was different from his other series because it was about a historical event that happened during Jacob's lifetime.

Migrant family. Photograph c. 1940. © Corbis-Bettmann.

"The migration gained in momentum." Panel 18 from *The Migration Series*, by Jacob Lawrence. 1940-41; text and title revised by the artist, 1993. Tempera on gesso on composition board. 18 x 12 in. Gift of Mrs. David M. Levy © Museum of Modern Art, New York/Photograph 2000.

"Migrants left. They did not feel safe. It was not wise to be found on the streets late at night. They were arrested on the slightest provocation." Panel 22 from *The Migration Series*, by Jacob Lawrence. 1940-41; text and title revised by the artist, 1993. Tempera on gesso on composition board. 12 x 18 in. Gift of Mrs. David M. Levy © Museum of Modern Art, New York/Photograph 2000.

The Migration Series tells the story of thousands of African-American families who left their homes in the southern United States and traveled North to cities like Chicago, Pittsburgh, and New York.

Although slavery had ended years before, many black people were still treated badly in the South. Black families traveled North

"They arrived in Pittsburgh, one of the great industrial centers of the North, in large numbers," Panel 45 from *The Migration Series*, by Jacob Lawrence. 1940-41. Tempera on masonite. 12 x 18 in. © Phillips Collection.

to look for jobs and a better life. In this series, Jacob showed how families lived in the South before moving North. He told of the hopes and struggles they had during their journey, and what happened when they arrived in the North.

"In the North the African American had freedom to vote," Panel 59 from *The Migration Series*, by Jacob Lawrence. 1940-41. Tempera on masonite. 11 1/2 x 17 1/2 in. © Phillips Collection.

The Black Migration was the largest group of people ever to move from one part of the United States to another. It's an event in American history that hardly anyone noticed was happening. Jacob Lawrence was one of the few people who recorded this important part of history.

"And the migration spread," Panel 23 from *The Migration Series,* by Jacob Lawrence. 1940-41. Tempera on masonite. 11 1/2 x 17 1/2 in. © Phillips Collection.

Jacob painted all sixty pictures of this series, color by color, at the same time. He wanted each painting to have a similar look. Jacob's wife, Gwen, helped him with the huge job. Gwen was an artist, too.

By the time Jacob Lawrence was thirty-two years old, he had become a very successful, well-known artist. But a strange thing happened. Instead of being happy about it, Jacob started feeling terrible. Suddenly, he started wondering if he really had any talent, or if maybe he had just been lucky. Most of his artist friends weren't doing nearly as well as he was.

This bothered him so much that he became nervous and depressed. Jacob decided to enter a hospital to treat his problem. After a few months, he felt better than ever. While he was in the hospital, Jacob painted scenes of other patients and activities around the hospital.

Depression, by Jacob Lawrence. 1950. Tempera on paper. 22 x 30 1/2 in. Gift of David M. Solinger.
© Whitney Museum of American Art/Photograph by Geoffrey Clements.

Jacob Lawrence went on to make paintings, prints, and giant murals. Workers were among his favorite subjects. He liked to show how builders cooperate to make things that are useful and important. This is what Jacob Lawrence hoped could happen everywhere, no matter what a person's job might be.

Pool Parlor, by Jacob Lawrence. 1942. Gouache on paper. 31 x 22 3/4 in. Arthur Hoppock Hearn Fund. © Metropolitan Museum of Art.

Builders 1980, Jacob Lawrence. 1980. Gouache on paper. 25 1/2 x 34 in. © Courtesy of the Artist and Francine Seders Gallery/Photograph by Chris Eden.

Jacob Lawrence in his Studio, 1994. Courtesy of the Artist and Francine Seders Gallery/Photograph by Spike Mafford.

Today Jacob Lawrence is known not only as a great artist, but as a storyteller, historian, and art teacher. Jacob's imaginative style of flat, colorful shapes makes his paintings seem filled with life.

Works of art in this book can be seen at the following places:

The Detroit Institute of Art, Detroit, Michigan
Francine Seders Gallery, Seattle, Washington
Hampton University Museum, Hampton, Virginia
The Metropolitan Museum of Art, New York, New York
The Museum of Modern Art, New York, New York
National Academy of Design, New York, New York
The Phillips Collection, Washington, D. C.
Smithsonian Institution, Hirshhorn Museum and Sculpture Garden, Washington, D.C.
Whitney Museum of American Art, New York, New York